Healing Wounds of Divorce:

The Breakdown that Led to My Breakthrough

Renee Jackson

Edited and Formatted by EditingByErica.com
Book Cover by Federica Dias

ISBN: 978-0-578-98511-4

CONTENTS

DEDICATION

To my beautiful Daughters Leah & Maya: Mommy loves you more than you'll ever know. Always remember to walk with your head high and your chin up. Your possibilities are endless. It's your world. I just live in it. :-)

Mommy: Thank you for always being the epitome of a strong Black woman. Thank you for your love, and all the lessons you've taught me. I miss our talks, but I'll treasure them and your wisdom forever!

Dooby: Thank you for always holding me down. I love you, bro!

To my entire sister circle, especially my chosen sisters Shanta and Chanti: Thank you for wrapping your arms around me and being the village that I need.

PROLOGUE

Divorce is one of the most horrific and painful experiences that anyone can ever go through. It can trigger a great deal of angst. Whether you've gone through a divorce or if you're in the process of going through one, you'll experience mixed emotions even if you were the one who initiated the process. Anyone who tells you that they felt nothing after their divorce is a bold face liar. In fact, the decision to divorce is daunting whether you're asking for one or being asked for one! No one ever gets married to get divorced so the thought of your marriage ending can be confusing, resulting in emotions such as anger, embarrassment, and guilt. It can also cause you to feel unloved, undesirable, rejected, and afraid that the pain will be never-ending. In fact, the pain you experience as a result of your divorce is often compared to the pain experienced when grieving the loss of a loved one. No two people will ever grieve the same, but the emotions you experience, and your actions thereafter will be a determining factor in how long you stay stuck in the grief.

When you stay stuck, you're not allowing yourself to move past the divorce. You may be shocked, in denial, angry, withdrawn or even telling anyone who will listen all the things your ex did wrong to "ruin" your marriage. All these coping strategies are natural and very real reactions and responses to the distress and disruption a divorce will cause you, but this won't allow you to live a peaceful, happy, and prosperous life after the divorce. If you're ever going to find peace and happiness, you must be intentional and be fully vested in the process of healing. I want to ask you this: Are you surviving or are you thriving? I ask because right after my divorce, I went into survival mode and truly didn't understand what it meant to thrive until I found my peace.

While no one can tell you how to heal and how long the process will be, you have to understand that change will require you to let go. You will have to begin thinking and moving differently to begin your healing process. Mindset is everything and it was my shift in mindset that eventually allowed me to focus on my healing, peace, and happiness. Everyone's journey is different and depending on what issues you're facing (infidelity, financial issues, property to split, child custody issues and/or other legal issues), your healing could also look different. No matter how strong you are, divorce can literally feel like the wind has been knocked out of you. But, like all great champions, you have to get back up and fight the good fight.

Divorce knocked me down but once I was done pretending that I was okay, I had to get back up. By no means was I ready to throw in the towel so I had to stop feeling sorry for myself, let go of the resentment, accept that I was now a divorced single mother, and use my experiences as a lesson. My divorce was truly the breakdown that led to my breakthrough! If you're looking for a book that will tell you all the things you want to hear, then this isn't the book for you. This book is for the person who is tired; tired of feeling broken, tired of wearing a mask and tired of allowing this one chapter in his or her life to define who they are. If you're ready to be intentional about your healing, then this is the book for you. By the time you finish reading this book, you should be ready to be intentional about healing your heart and finding your peace to live a happy and prosperous life.

CHAPTER 1:
THE UGLY TRUTH:
Acknowledge & accept your feelings.

"There are some people who will be content with just 'being' but some of us that God has chosen, we have to be 'broken.' We have to get sick. We have to lose a job. We have to go through divorce. We have to bury our spouse, parents, best friend, or our child because, in those moments of desperation, God is breaking us but when the breaking is done, then we will be able to see the reason for which we were created." - *Unknown Author*

In 2017 I had reached a breaking point. My mom had suffered a severe stroke which left her paralyzed and unable to speak. Initially I was in denial, but then reality set in and I was struggling to come to terms with the fact that this would be my mother's state. I went from speaking to my mom two and three times a day to never hearing her voice again. I was operating on autopilot and really struggling with all that was going on in my life. I've always been a strong friend and the one person that everyone has been able to depend on. However, the girl that seemed unbreakable was definitely breaking and I felt too ashamed to even talk to anyone about it! I was losing it; losing my faith, losing my fight and my marriage was crumbling! Never in a million years would I have ever pictured that my life would turn out the way it did. It seemed like one moment I was married to my best friend and the next moment we were calling it quits. I was spiraling and felt like I could no longer pretend to keep it all together.

Have you ever heard people say, "They're only alive because of their children?" Well, that was me! I didn't know it at the time, but I was experiencing anxiety, depression, and passive suicidal ideation. Every time the thought of no longer wanting to live crept up on me, the thoughts of my daughters became stronger. I remember talking to my then husband and telling him that I felt like my mental health was off. He laughed at me, told me "I was crazy" and that nothing was wrong with me. Since then, I've learned to forgive him. I had to learn that if he knew better, he would have reacted better, but I resented him for that comment. It was one of the reasons I fell out of love with him. He was the one person that I was hoping would save me. How could he not notice? I struggled with finding the strength to do anything. I would go to work, come home, and lock myself in the room, having only the desire to sleep. This went on for months before I built up the courage and willpower to seek professional help. This was ultimately the best decision that I could have ever made. I've always been so quick to save everyone else, but I started fighting to save myself.

While seeking therapy for my depression, I was also struggling with the fluctuation of my weight, which was something that my ex often criticized me for. See, the thing about depression is that it plays tricks on you. I wanted to work out and I wanted to be fit, but my depression told me otherwise. My battle with depression took every ounce of motivation out of me. I tried to get my ex to understand this struggle, so much so that I even took him to one of my therapy sessions so that he could hear about my experience from a professional. It helped a little, but the damage was already done. We were drifting apart, and I was losing the energy and desire to even give my marriage a chance to survive. However, I also knew I was afraid to lose my husband, the life we built together and what I had come to embrace as "normal." We began to have all of these talks which never really led to any resolve. Marriage counseling didn't even work because at one point I noticed I was the only one putting forth effort to fix us. I was breaking my own self down in trying to save my marriage. If I was going to beat depression, I had to put on my oxygen mask and save myself!

For some reason, neither one of us wanted to make the move towards asking for a divorce, but eventually we decided to do a trial separation. This led to very little resolve because we still had to see each other every day when he took our daughter to school. It was also tough explaining to my daughters why their dad wasn't sleeping at home or if and when he would return. One part of me was fighting for my marriage and the other part gave up. One thing is certain: I do believe that what's meant to be will be and what isn't will be shown to you in due time.

The day we started our separation, I somehow knew it was the end, but as I watched him leave, I was still praying for some divine sign on whether I was making the right decision. The separation gave me some time to be still and pray hard. When I got tired of praying, I kept praying and trying to seek the answers that I needed. We continued marriage counseling, but between those sessions and my individual sessions I started showing up for me. I was coming to terms with the fact that my ex was now a stranger to me and that our time together was up. I accepted what was and built up the courage to discuss the option of divorce.

We were initially amicable but as I was preparing myself to live a life without the only man that I thought I would spend the rest of my life with, I found out about his indiscretions. This shifted the whole dynamic, as I grew deep rooted resentment. If "fake it until you make it" was a person, that was me! I was angry, not sleeping and extremely stressed. I felt like the devil was just busy! I was lost and didn't know where to turn, but I was in denial and couldn't accept my reality. I was operating in brokenness and felt utter embarrassment that my marriage failed and was coming to an end. You see, the thing about stress is that it will manifest itself in different forms and can negatively impact your life in so many ways, including mind, body, and spirit. Unfortunately, I wasn't able to wear the mask for long. Throughout this process, I was literally having breakdowns at work in the bathroom, coming home and only having enough energy to feed and bathe my children. I was emotionally disconnected from everyone! I was heartbroken, bitter, and falling into an even deeper state of depression.

Months went on and I was still heartbroken and feeling sorry for myself. I kept telling everyone that I was okay, but I'm sure they knew I wasn't. My ex was still allowed in the home we created together in an effort to keep things "normal" for our kids. However, all that did was ignite my anxiety, and I started feeling like a stranger in my own home when he was around. On top of that, I was still trying to accept my divorce, and heal my broken heart. New Year's Eve 2018 was a turning point for me. I was listening to a pastor give a sermon and I felt like he was speaking to me! He mentioned that the new year would bring in some powerful and great things in my life, but I had to make room by letting go of what no longer served me any purpose. I suddenly realized that when I thought the devil was so busy destroying my life, it was actually God disrupting my life to prepare me for something greater!

I realized that I had to come to terms with my marriage ending and just let it go. If I was going to do that, I knew I needed to set some boundaries, and also create a new normal for my daughters. It became clear that God needed to break my heart in order to save my soul. I had become too complacent with being the "ride or die" wife and also lost myself in being a mother. I accepted the fact that everything happens for a reason and that I was chosen to be gracefully broken in order to be who I was truly meant to be.

Sometimes when the chips are falling, we just have to let them fall and stop being so consumed with saving what we shouldn't. As women we are quick to go to war for our men, our children, our parents and even our careers, so much so that we neglect to go to war for ourselves. Healing looks different for everyone, and you may be at a different point in your journey than other readers. If you're ready to do the work and go to war for yourself then you have to be intentional and most of all be honest, especially with yourself. Sometimes in order to start our journey of healing we have to get uncomfortable and momentarily be okay with not being okay.

I won't lie and say my life took a major 180° turn from the moment I surrendered to not being okay, but once I stopped pretending, I felt so much lighter and was ready to push forward. Denial, pride, hurt, and shame kept me stuck for too long. It kept me pretending that I was okay when I wasn't. ***The first step I took to healing my heart was admitting that I wasn't okay. I had to actually accept it, and say, "I'm not okay."***

Ask yourself: *What is keeping me stuck? What is the first step I will take on my journey of healing?*

CHAPTER 2:

LETTING GO:

Acknowledge & accept that resentment is keeping you stuck.

"Resentment is like a drug or a cancerous tumor. Once it takes root, it will eventually spread like a wildfire and eat away at your soul. As soon as you feel the resentment growing and spreading, uproot it and sow the seeds of something more positive." -Renee Jackson

I tried accepting that my marriage ended, but I couldn't shake the thoughts of how it ended. My divorce was having a profound impact on my life and the resentment I was harboring towards my ex was growing and growing. It continued to manifest itself in the form of anxiety. Being around my ex would cause me to feel physically ill. This is an unfortunate but very real side effect of allowing resentment to take a toll on you. Resentment is closely linked to anger, and is a combination of negative thoughts, feelings and ill will towards someone or something linked to situations or issues from the past. Some people even say that developing and maintaining resentment towards someone causes you to mentally become their slave, both emotionally and spiritually. On the outside, I appeared to be happy to no longer be in an unhappy marriage, but on the inside I was dead.

You see history is what actually kept me harboring resentment for way too long! The more time you spend thinking about what happened, why it happened, and all of the "should've, could've and would'ves" the more the bondage of resentment will grow. I dismissed many things early on in my relationship. I felt like I had sacrificed so much for my marriage, so how did I end up here? Now, I've heard older women say, "Once a cheater, always a cheater, so don't allow it." But is it really something that you "allow?" I think for many people who are faced with infidelity, you chose to get through it for different reasons. When it first happened in our relationship, honestly, I was a young hot head. Yes, I was hurt, but I felt like we had been together all of this time so why would I leave now? I thought I had invested so much already, and I wasn't about to allow another woman to have what was mine! I think that was the worst decision of my life, as I never took the time to heal that hurt nor was the trust in our relationship rebuilt. This was definitely also indicative of my lack of self-love and inability to hold him accountable.

I think from then on, I just adopted the motto, "A man will be a man so let him be." I can't say that I'm 100% accurate, but me staying is probably what contributed it to happening again. I was afraid to break up the family my kids had, and I was afraid to let go of all the history that was shared. Unfortunately, that was when my resentment grew, and I never truly dealt with it but going through a divorce caused it to resurface.

I knew that our divorce meant not only would I be letting go of my husband, but I'd also be letting go of our friendship that I valued more than anything in the world. Ultimately while trying to cope, I inadvertently became stoic. I'm not sure if you've ever experienced this but you become numb, resisting the urge to feel, and becoming hardened as a result of the hurt and pain someone has caused you. In addition to all the issues you may experience within, resentment can have a gruesome impact on your other relationships. I often lashed out towards others.

I didn't know what peace would look or feel like, but I knew that what I was living in wasn't it! It took me a long time to acknowledge it, but I was done faking it. I started going to war for myself! I learned that resentment thrives on your negative actions, thoughts, and emotions. For far too long I allowed history to keep me stuck thinking about the past when I should've been thinking about myself and my own healing. I had to realize that some people are seasonal, and while they may be a part of your history, they may have never been meant to be a part of your future. This meant I had to let it all go for my own sanity and peace. ***The second step in healing my heart was understanding that change isn't easy. Change is messy and confusing but staying stuck on history and***

operating out of resentment is messier. I had to release the resentment I was harboring for my own sake.

Ask yourself: *What am I holding on to? What will letting it go do for me?*

CHAPTER 3:
DISRUPTION IS NEVER ACCIDENTAL:
Acknowledge & accept the loss.

"God does not disrupt or dismantle your life by accident. Whether you know your purpose or not, just know that God will never break you down without building you back up. Everything that happens in your life, will prepare you to be a greater you." - Renee Jackson

I had prayed for peace and somehow, I wasn't getting it. Months after I separated from my husband, I struggled with adjusting to my new life and I was still having a pity party for myself. I don't think I completely accepted that being a divorcee would be my new normal. I couldn't understand why all of this had to happen to me. I thought, "I'm a good woman, I was a good wife, I didn't sign up to be a single mom. How on Earth did I end up here?" Let's be real, who gets married to the love of their life with the intent of it not being successful? I was angry with God, I was angry with myself, I was hating my ex and I was just simply hurt! By no means did I want my ex back, but the idea of no longer being married and the idea of losing my best friend wasn't sitting well with me. To also know how we ended was disrupting my entire mind and spirit.

Adjusting to this new life meant that because we had children, there would be times that we would occupy the same space but learning to control my emotions and words around him was tough. There was so much tension, and quite a few disagreements, but I knew I didn't want my children to grow up thinking that this was the right way! I started holding in my feelings which also wasn't healthy. Falling asleep at night was the worst. I couldn't even sleep alone. For the first few months of our separation my kids slept in the same bed with me, where my youngest would cry often for her dad. I watched as my oldest became my protector. Somehow, she became so consumed with whether I was okay that she was masking her feelings about all of it. Although they didn't know it, I needed the comfort of my children just as much as they needed mine, but I also felt like I had to keep it together for them.

I knew if I wanted to fully heal, change needed to happen. I had to let go and let God, because ruminating on the "whys" and "what ifs" was draining, both mentally and physically. One night after a crazy day at work and just being on an emotional roller coaster, I got down on my knees and prayed. I cried and prayed and cried and prayed some more. I don't know what it was, but this calm feeling came over me and I heard a voice say, "Be still, but keep going." I know that's such an oxymoron, but it makes so much sense to me now. I felt like God was sending me a message saying that I may be in a dark place, but I needed to trust his process. That's exactly what I did; I gave it to God and started focusing on my continued healing. I stopped worrying and started focusing on me.

I started communicating with my ex, ONLY about our kids and changed my whole mindset. Since high school, he had been my confidant, lover, and friend so naturally my default was to want to talk to him. I had to not only divorce him as the husband who broke my heart, but as the best friend that betrayed me. This helped our communication as I started realizing you can't control the actions of others, only how you react to them. I was calmer and growing more as a woman. As I prayed more, I started having more positive thoughts. Although I felt like God broke me down, he was slowly but surely building me back up. He started preparing me for a greater and more powerful purpose, proving that disruption is never accidental.

What many people don't know is that going through a divorce or breakup is like being on a rollercoaster; there will be so many loops, swoops, twists, turns, ups and downs. Thus, you'll experience various emotions like denial, anger, bargaining and sadness. However, trying not to deal with the different emotions will eat away at your soul and destroy your peace. If you're really committed to your healing, an emotion that you should seek is acceptance: Acceptance of what has happened and the ability to move on. So, like grieving the loss of a loved one, you must come to terms with your marriage ending, grieve it and move on. ***The third step in healing was letting go of what was and accepting what is to come.***

Ask yourself: *From this moment on, what do I commit to accepting for the sake of my own healing?*

CHAPTER 4:
FIXING YOUR OWN TOXICITY:
Acknowledge & accept that forgiveness is for you.

"Forgiveness is not forgetting; it is simply denying your pain the right to control your life." -Iyanla Vanzant

For as long as I can remember, I have always been a person who holds grudges and I struggled with forgiving. To be fully transparent, this stems from issues that I've dealt with in the past from my father and my struggle to learn the importance of forgiveness. However, that's a story I'll tell in another book. For far too long I allowed my unwillingness to forgive people to keep me broken, constantly operating as a victim and captive to those who have wronged me. I didn't quite understand how I could truly forgive if I couldn't forget. It was easy to verbalize that I forgave someone if they had wronged me, but I don't think I ever truly learned the power and essence of practicing forgiveness until I made the conscious decision to be intentional about it.

Whether we like it or not, life happens and unfortunately, we are not and can never be responsible for someone's actions or the trials that life will throw at us. However, what we can control is our own unwillingness to forgive. Although I had expressed my forgiveness to my ex, I was lying to him and most importantly I was lying to myself. I knew I hadn't forgiven him because I was bothered by his presence, the sound of his name and was stuck on how he wronged me, dismissing the part I played in everything. You'll know you've truly forgiven someone when you feel at peace with what happened, and for me that wasn't the case.

The issue wasn't me staying stuck on the idea of my marriage ending, but I was still harboring malice towards my ex for the pain he had caused me. I wanted him to feel the pain I felt but I didn't realize that the one person I was hurting the most by refusing to forgive was myself. My resistance to forgive turned into bitterness and I became toxic. If there's any emotion to be feared it's bitterness and like resentment, it too can eat away at your soul! If we're not careful, bitterness can eventually grow and manifest in negative ways. At one point in all of our lives there will be someone or something that will cause bitterness to grow in our hearts, but until we commit to change, we'll only be harming ourselves. Once I got real with myself, and intentional about forgiving, I experienced happiness and felt more at peace. I had finally started grasping the concept that, "The key to openness, the door to healing and life after divorce, is forgiveness."[1]

As I began working on forgiveness, I realized that first and foremost I needed to forgive myself. I had to take accountability and forgive myself for the role I played in the demise of my marriage including how harshly I spoke when I was upset. I felt guilty for not keeping my family together, for staying as long as I did knowing that I was unhappy, and not loving myself enough to recognize that my expectations in my marriage were based on a false reality. It's so ironic how much grace and mercy we bestow upon others but are unwilling to grant it to ourselves. While forgiving won't erase the memories and the hurt, it most definitely will set you free.

The moment you choose to forgive, you're reclaiming your power. Once you commit to making the conscious decision to wake up every day and work on forgiving yourself and those who have wronged you, the more you'll understand that you're making room for your own blessings and closure. In her book Don't Settle for Safe, Sarah Jakes Roberts mentions the importance of not allowing closure to be contingent upon our willingness to forgive. Therefore, forgiveness involves understanding that sometimes our pain is necessary for our growth, and is never about the other person, but the "reconciliation with oneself." Allow yourself to process this for a moment!

Be honest with yourself at this very moment. Who are

you struggling to forgive? What are you struggling to forgive yourself for? I understand it's hard to forgive but it's possible. You can't expect peace if you're not willing to forgive, so start now. Life is too precious, and time waits for no one. Commit and stay committed to releasing what you're holding on to. You have to understand that you're human. Give yourself some compassion, and let it go. Every day you should wake up and state what or who you're forgiving and why it's important. It was this habitual and intentional daily routine that allowed me to truly forgive myself and my ex.

I had to understand that the longer I was unwilling to forgive, the longer I would be stuck in this same cycle. Yes, it is absolutely hard, and right now you may not be ready to do so but just know that it's not impossible. No one on this planet is perfect and I'm sure there's been a time or two that you had to ask someone else for forgiveness. We must also realize that sometimes the way in which others treat us is never about us, it's usually about them, their brokenness and/or insecurities. Hence, hurt or broken people often hurt others. It is up to them to right their wrongs for their sake, but you absolutely need to forgive for your sake!

To be transparent, forgiveness doesn't mean that you'll stop feeling the hurt or that you'll forget what caused your pain, but it is an important part of your healing process. Although I had chosen to forgive, I still maintained clear boundaries between my ex and myself. Those boundaries and my choice to forgive were crucial to my healing process. When you commit to forgiving, you'll slowly notice that the resentment, bitterness, and anger will disappear. This process wasn't easy for me, but I know that since my peace and happiness was what I was striving for then I needed to forgive. Whenever those negative thoughts or feelings started to resurface, I reflected on how far I had come and why unforgiveness wasn't an option.

Healing is a process that can ultimately transform and contribute to a better life, but without your willingness to forgive, this transformation will never take form. Forgiveness is what truly saved me. **If you're serious about moving on and finding your peace and happiness, then start with forgiveness. This was a major step for me in healing after divorce.** The power of forgiveness is a mighty one but once you're able to go through each stage, you're a step closer to healing your heart.

Taking the necessary steps to forgive will include:

1. Acknowledging that forgiveness needs to take place.
2. Identifying who or what you need to forgive and why.
3. Forgiving yourself in the process
4. Recognizing that forgiveness requires intentionality; It won't happen by just saying it. You must practice forgiveness.

[1]Myles Munroe, *Single Married Separated And Life After Divorce Daily Study.* (United States: Destiny Image Publishers, 2004), 31.

CHAPTER 5:
LEAN ON YOUR CRUTCH:
Acknowledge & accept that you'll need support.

"Sometimes, asking for help is the most meaningful example of self-reliance." -Unknown

The gift and curse of being an '80s baby (as I like to call myself) is that many of us grew up with some strong and empowered women in our corner. The one thing that most of these women didn't teach us, my mother included, is the importance of dealing with our emotions or working on them by seeking help when we need it, specifically professional help. In fact, seeking help and learning how to increase emotional intelligence requires a level of vulnerability that takes courage and is the epitome of strength. I grew up watching my mother do her best to mask her emotions. I truly admired her strength but what I needed most that she didn't teach me was the capacity to be conscious of my emotions as well as how to effectively control and express them. I learned to never let anyone, especially a man, see me cry, break a sweat or feel like I needed them. While I was building my hard exterior, I started suffering in complete silence. While I didn't want to be in my marriage anymore, I don't think I was content with the idea that I'd now be a single divorced mother. I know that sounds crazy and makes no sense at all, but the reality is when you're in a relationship with someone for so long you become dependent on them. We were best friends since high school, shared a lot of experiences together and had two kids who would also be affected by our split.

I was struggling to cope, and I truly felt like I would die from a broken heart. That may not sound logical, but "Broken Heart Syndrome" is a real thing. In fact, women are more likely to be affected by this than men as a result of a sudden emotionally stressful event like divorce, a breakup, or loss of a loved one. I couldn't eat, I barely slept, and I had mentally checked out. I was simply existing and operating in survival mode. Living in this state is unstable and brutally dangerous. I felt like because I went from being a wife to being a single mother that I didn't have time to feel or process my emotions. My motto was,

"I have two daughters who need me to be strong for them. Being weak is not an option." As a result, I went on for months without processing my feelings about the end of my marriage and I was suffering.

Unfortunately, the way in which I was dealing with my divorce didn't work out too well. On several occasions I allowed my emotions to cause me to lash out at others. It was either that or a shut down. I did a lot of masking my emotions and telling everyone I was fine. Only my close friends and a few family members knew what was going on. I started buying all of these self-help books and following people on social media who had faced similar experiences. I thought I was doing a decent job of hiding my emotions and healing on my own, but the joke was on me!

Lack of emotional intelligence and denial can affect the way in which you communicate and process what you're feeling. While I knew I wasn't okay, I was afraid to seek or even accept help. I didn't want to appear to be weak because I've always been the go-to person for many, and I was taught to be strong. I also didn't want anyone to think I was "crazy" for seeking help, a stigma that many women who are taught to be strong struggle with, specifically in the Black community. But what happens when the girl who seemed unbreakable finally breaks? The outcome is gut-wrenching and downright ugly!

Once I stopped kidding myself and others, I committed to being more open during my therapy sessions. I didn't know that years and years of not dealing with my feelings is what caused me to develop a severe case of anxiety and depression. During therapy I was tapping into all of these feelings. Slowly but surely, I began learning how to develop and improve my emotional intelligence. Therapy also allowed me to deal with the issues I hadn't faced in my marriage, but I was still stuck in a cycle of brokenness. In order to get past it I needed more help than what my therapist was able to provide. I stumbled upon a great divorce coach by accident and eventually signed up. This was a game changer for me! The irony is that she actually reached out to me on social media after she noticed I attended her live recordings each week. It's interesting that this stranger could tell that I needed help. It was an experience that pushed me in ways that I didn't want but definitely needed.

Without divorce coaching, I would still be lying to myself and everyone else by pretending that nothing was wrong and acting as if my marriage ending had no effect on my emotional being. In fact, that was the total opposite. It affected me so much that I was becoming physically sick. Coaching allowed me to get real with myself, take accountability, level up and be mature. It was this shift from being focused on my marriage ending to now focusing on myself that made the experience worthwhile. All too often people stay stuck and are unable to heal after a divorce because their primary focus is the other individual rather than themselves. Well, I had to get over everything that I felt my ex did wrong to focus on how I was going to heal and commit to my own happiness and peace. I wasn't about to sit and stay stuck focusing on my ex when there was so much more to life.

In order to get through the pain, hurt, embarrassment and shame I was feeling I had to process my emotions. As I have previously mentioned, everyone's journey and path look different but the one commonality that remains is that ***healing takes commitment and work.*** In order to commit to my healing, I had to do the work. This meant that I had to face my hurt and even sit in it as a part of the process. It was scary, messy, and frustrating but one that I needed to go through. You're not going to like it, but it's necessary to heal your heart and get past the hurt. The key is to not stay stuck in it. It's true that you're able to mask your pain for some time, but after a while it will start to weigh on you and show up in other ways. Once you get through it (because you will), you'll come out stronger.

Each week the sessions with my divorce coach were recorded. At the end of my time with her I went back to watch the recordings. I cried at the sight of the initial recording because I couldn't recognize myself. I looked worn down, my skin had broken out and I looked lost. As the weeks progressed, I noticed a shift in my appearance: Clearer skin, smiles, and much more energy. I promise there's always a light at the end of the tunnel! For many like myself, I needed a little support to see that light.

There are very few people who have successfully healed after a divorce without the support of others. If you don't do what's needed to heal, you'll constantly operate in a state of brokenness. How do I know? I know because that was me. I had to get real with myself and seek all the professional help that I could get and not be ashamed of it. It was this pivotal experience that made me stronger and allowed me to focus more on myself rather than the divorce or how angry I was at my ex. Oftentimes, women stay stuck after their divorce because they're so focused on the divorce or their ex that they're not able to focus on themselves. Yes, divorce can be devastating but because it is a life altering experience, you will need to spend more time focused on you if you truly want to heal your heart.

Going through a divorce will require you to have the right people supporting you. Unfortunately, you may find that in order to heal you may need to separate from those who aren't empathetic, understanding and supportive.

Think about it for a moment: When someone breaks a leg the doctor will often require them to use a crutch or two for support. Similarly, in order to have the right support on your journey, you may need to lean on a person or two who will be genuine and healthy for your mental and emotional well-being. I can attest to the benefits of leaning on healthy crutches for support after a divorce. I stress the importance of your crutch being healthy because you will have to discern who is there to truly support you and whether that support will be detrimental.

Here are some healthy crutches that you may find useful:

- Friends and family, specifically those who have experienced a divorce or are understanding & non-judgmental
- Faith
- Hobbies you enjoy
- Therapy
- Divorce Coaching
- Support Groups

In order to seek help, you're going to have to push your pride aside and trust the process. Part of trusting the process is trusting that there are people who can support you through it. Do not allow the idea of "being strong" or "it's nobody's business" to keep you from getting the support you need. These are generational preconceived notions that too many women have struggled with, me included. Truthfully, it will be a scary and uncomfortable experience, but worth it once you come out on the other side. I'm not telling you to seek professional support, as this may or may not be something you believe in, but it did wonders for me. You will however have to find the right crutch and solid support system to help get you through.

Once I was ready to focus on breaking generational curses to find my own peace and happiness, I saw evolution within myself. It doesn't make you weak, it actually shows that you're strong and giving yourself grace. The fifth step to healing is being committed to seeking help; we all can use and benefit from support, especially if you notice your healing is stagnant.

CHAPTER 6:
EMBRACE YOUR SINGLENESS:
Acknowledge and accept the season you're in.

"To fall in love with yourself is the first secret to happiness." -Robert Morley

Falling in love can be one of the most daunting experiences ever but simultaneously, it can also be amazing. Imagine what it feels like when you fall in love with yourself. It's a feeling of bliss and the greatest step you can ever take towards healing and finding your own happiness. Falling in love with yourself doesn't happen overnight. In fact, you have to wake up every day and make a conscious decision to choose you and love yourself. You must be willing to make that investment in yourself once you decide to come to terms with embracing your singleness.

After my divorce I had to commit to falling in love with myself and embrace my season of singleness. When I initially became a divorcee, I felt lonely and out of place when attending weddings and other social events or even being around friends who were couples. It felt impossible to do these things as a single woman. I didn't want to be faced with the stares, questions, or judgment about being newly divorced or single. As a result, I turned down invites and avoided many events for fear of being ostracized. Most of this was me being dramatic and feeling insecure about being single. Divorce is one of the most devastating experiences I think I've ever endured as a woman but coming to terms with being single was just as hard.

Embracing your singleness is crucial to the healing process. You need time first and foremost for you, and secondly to focus on the people you do have in your life. Use this time to reconnect with your friends and family. If you have children, use this time to build greater bonds and relationships with them. Do all the things that you desire to do, traveling, reading, going on outings alone, exercising and working on your health, fixing your finances, and building generational wealth. As time passes, you'll become more comfortable with being alone, and no longer feel lonely or insecure about being single.

Dating can be fun too but be sure that you're truly ready, otherwise you risk making the mistake of getting into a "situationship" or relationship too quickly. I have heard so many people say the best way to get over the end of a marriage is to put yourself out there, but is this really a long-term solution? From personal experience I know that's not the answer! Breakups can be hard and even harder to heal from but dating or getting into another relationship too soon due to the "quick fix" approach is unhealthy. This usually results in rebound relationships and hurting a new partner. Staying committed to your healing can help you avoid such situations.

I was quickly able to tell that I was dating too soon after my divorce when someone was trying to get me to commit to a relationship. The idea of being wanted, catered to and treated better than I've ever been was amazing, but what he wanted me to reciprocate, I knew I couldn't give. I decided early on that dating wasn't something I was ready for until I had done the work to completely heal. What most women would long for in a man was right in front of me, but I was too broken to receive it. Although I was transparent about where I was on my journey, I'm sure I ended up hurting this person in the process. I had no business dating and made a promise to myself to focus on my healing, rather than being a heartbreaker. When we haven't fully healed after a breakup, we often date to fulfill our feelings of inadequacy or loneliness rather than dating because we truly want to date.

Don't ever think dating will help you heal faster; it'll actually stunt your growth and healing process. Allow your singleness to liberate you and focus on finding peace. After a breakup, the person who stays single and works on their healing will often be better off, emotionally and mentally. There's a good chance that you need to unpack some emotional trauma that you've experienced. If you don't know who you are after going through a divorce or breakup, then getting romantically involved with someone won't be beneficial. While you may feel a temporary satisfaction, that feeling will subside. I can't stress enough the importance of taking time to focus on yourself. I promise there's nothing wrong with being single, but you have to learn to be content with or without a partner. Ultimately, you'll build a happier life and when you're ready, you'll be able to fully focus on a new and healthy relationship.

I hope you understand you are worthy of love, but it starts with self-love. Self-love is the greatest love of all, so breathe and focus on yourself during this time. Fall in love with yourself so deeply that you are committed to your happiness without feeling guilty about it. This sounds good and you may be thinking it is easier said than done, but it can be done. Once I made peace with my singleness, the love I developed for myself became invigorating and empowering. To be clear, I've always been empowered, but this newfound love allowed me to become my own best friend and make myself happy. Sometimes we get so caught up in our love for our significant other and how they make us feel that we become dependent on that connection, rather than cultivating that within ourselves. We're not taught that it's actually our job to make ourselves happy and to love ourselves before we expect this from others.

Back when my ex and I first separated I was so afraid to be alone that when it was his time with our children, I felt lost and would fall apart. I missed and longed for companionship and truly didn't understand how to depend on myself or even know how to be myself. I knew how lonely I felt in my marriage but being single felt worse. I truly didn't know how to be happy as a single woman. Eventually I started understanding that being single was my chance to embrace and get to know the woman that I had become because in all honesty, I wasn't the woman I once was. I started loving myself so much that I snatched my power back and the game changed! My self-esteem increased and the way in which I started to value myself more than ever. Now I appreciate time to myself as it gives me an opportunity to do all of the things I wanted to do or never had the time to do. Although I am open to the possibility of love and falling in love, I can truly say that I am content with being single. I may be alone but by no means am I lonely. Once you know this it will make a significant difference!

Please don't allow your season of singleness to keep you down. Brighter days are ahead! I urge you to manifest all of the dreams and goals you hope to make a reality. Unlock those dormant aspirations that have been laying low and waiting to come out. As women, we often become so consumed with being wives, girlfriends, or mothers that we rarely do what makes us happy. As a married woman you were probably used to doing almost everything as a couple, so much so that you've probably forgotten all of the things you like to do. You may even be struggling with who you've become. It's interesting that women more so than men will give up their individuality when they get married, then if their marriage ends, they don't know who they are as women. Well, getting to know yourself and doing what you like to do is going to help you be the best version of you. Work on exploring what you need, your wants, what you like, what you don't like and your goals. **No matter where you are on your journey, I want to encourage you to work on this sixth step:** Embrace your singleness and do what sets your soul on fire.

Ask yourself: *What do I love about myself? What can I do to make myself happy?*

CHAPTER 7:
HEAL AND MOVE ON:
Acknowledge & accept that pain may still exist, but it shouldn't define you.

"Don't be so happy thriving off of pain that you forget happiness is an option." - Unknown

My singleness left an uncertainty most women experience when they go through a breakup or a divorce. I had done the work to heal my heart but there was still a void I was feeling. I started thinking about all of the obstacles that had been thrown at me and how I've never let them deter me from doing what I wanted to do. Once I started reflecting on my accomplishments, I knew God was calling me to woman up and level up. That unsettling feeling I experienced was on purpose. I had to recognize that at this point in my life, the only person I'm in competition with is myself! In order to walk into this next chapter of my life that I'm authoring, I had to deal with myself, be intentional and take accountability.

I began to realize that being single didn't make me inadequate! What I needed most was to focus on being the best and most authentic version of myself. After being with one person for so long, I almost didn't know who I was as a woman. This meant I couldn't seek anything from a man, unless I worked on me. Working on myself had its benefits. I needed to break in order to be intentional for myself and my kids. Most importantly I realized that I am a woman first and owe it to myself to live happily. Being married or with a man wasn't going to define me.

Aside from dealing with my mother's sickness, divorce was one of the most difficult and heartbreaking experiences I've gone through. It changed my life and above all, my sense of self. I had to put on my big girl pants and focus on rebuilding myself. Lastly, I had to build my confidence, which was shattered into a million pieces. Everything about divorce has the potential to break you down, stripping you of every bit of sense of self you've ever had. For this reason, becoming the best version of yourself will require you to keep your chin up, head held high and remain determined. You'll need to be courageous and take steps to rebuild yourself. For me this meant building my self-worth, identifying my values, and rediscovering my true purpose in life. Don't get me wrong, I had hobbies and things I was passionate about but so many women make the mistake of confusing their passions with their purpose. Sometimes it is during our darkest moments or toughest storms we've weathered that we discover our true purpose!

To discover your true purpose, you're going to have to build your confidence and commit to your goals and dreams. Never forget that you are in control of only you. You're the CEO of your life. Do things that make you content and happy. This will require developing a routine that is right for you. This could include but is not limited to, picking up new skills or hobbies, developing a new self-care routine, traveling, working out, reading, going back to school, and simply celebrating you.

While everyone will need to do what's best for them, doing nothing leaves absolutely no room for growth. Building confidence for myself meant maintaining healthy mental & physical health patterns, and continued expressions of gratitude for everything that was positive and going right in my life. I had to focus on building my self-confidence and the internal work instead of the external like hair and nails. Don't get me wrong, what woman doesn't love to pamper herself?? However, if I didn't focus on my inner core first, I knew I wouldn't develop the self-confidence needed to be comfortable and happy with my authentic self.

Too many people spend time focused on their outer appearances, but when they're stripped of the hair, nails, and fashion, they're unhappy and have very little confidence in themselves. Think about it: So many celebrities appear to have it all, from fame and money, to perfect bodies. Reality is, most of them are unfulfilled and probably some of the most insecure individuals. This wasn't going to ever be me!

In building my confidence I also developed an abundance of self-love and a strong value system. Life can have profound meaning and be unique to each individual. Everyone will develop their own understanding of what it should be. The life you make for yourself after divorce is truly contingent upon what's most important to you. For me, life after divorce meant never going back to what broke me and never allowing anything or anyone to disrupt my peace. Although a monkey wrench was thrown at my life and what I thought would be my forever, I couldn't let it define me. I started viewing my divorce as a way to get in touch with all that I felt disconnected to.

As I went on this journey of healing, I was so focused on myself that I forgot my children were hurting too. I had to commit to being genuinely happy if I wanted my kids to prosper. If you have children, you need to understand that the longer you stay stuck in your own hurt, the longer it will take for your children to heal. Sometimes we're so absorbed with and blinded by our own hurt that we don't realize our children are hurting as well. As previously mentioned, I wasn't taught the fundamentals or provided with the tools needed to healthily process or express my emotions, so I owed it to my kids to provide not only financially but emotionally too. Being genuinely happy and keeping my kids happy means the world to me. Once our family dynamics changed, I had to provide my children the space they needed to express their emotions while not being so consumed with my own. I worked on building a greater connection with them. The bond we share now is deeply valued and could never be replaced.

What I took for granted or didn't give enough attention to, I now value more than ever: My happiness, my peace, my sanity, and kids. I also built greater and deeper connections with my friends, which were lost somewhere along the way during my marriage. The time and energy I spent feeling sorry for myself was now spent on loving myself and developing a deeper understanding of myself as a woman, mother, and friend. I made a promise that in order to stay true to myself I had to do what kept me aligned to my personal values, goals and spiritual beliefs.

I hope that by now you are feeling confident and ready to commit to your healing, finding your peace and your happiness. Always remember that only you are in control of you, so don't ever be defined by a mate or feel like your marriage ending means your life did too. You haven't failed and you certainly deserve to be happy. Spend this season working on being the absolute best version of you. Be very meticulous about where and to whom you allocate your time. Going through a divorce is one of the most humbling experiences I've ever endured. It sucked so much energy from me and brought me down to my knees. Although it's something I would never wish on my worst enemy, it also brought me to where I am now, and I probably would go through it again if I had to. Crazy right? Well, it was that breakdown that led to my breakthrough! After all the crying, anger and feeling sorry for myself I had to be committed to change and walk in my purpose.

There's no wrong or right way to discover your purpose and more than likely you'll discover that what your purpose was during your marriage doesn't look the same now that you're divorced. I know because this was me! I remember going through divorce coaching and admitting that I lost myself and no longer knew who I was when I looked in the mirror. When I think about how I looked during my first session with the divorce coach, it brought tears to my eyes. I looked so beat down. I wore all of my heartbreak, defeat and confusion on my face. Divorce coaching gave me hope, and the push I truly needed. At that point it was me against me. I am not that same woman and could have never imagined that I would be where I am now. Every now and again I revisit that video, to give myself a reminder of what I never want to go back to.

Rediscovering or finding your purpose is a process and definitely won't happen overnight. However, by becoming more self-aware, identifying your goals, dreams, life experiences and what motivates you, you'll get closer to what is meant for you. There may be things in your life that you are passionate about but be careful. Don't be so focused on your passions that you confuse them with your purpose!

Grab a pen and paper! Let's answer some questions that will get you started on finding your purpose:

Self- Awareness

1. What were your goals as a child? Do they align with who you are now?
2. What are your strengths? Talents? Abilities?
3. Which of your attributes or traits are the strongest?

Motivation

1. What invigorates you or sets your soul on fire?
2. What are you most passionate about?
3. What are you most proud of and why?
4. When and where are you mostly inspired?

CHAPTER 8:
TURN YOUR PAIN INTO PURPOSE:
Acknowledge & accept the breakdown that led to your breakthrough.

"Sometimes what didn't work out for you, indeed worked out for you." – Unknown

Another moment of truth I'll share is that I thought life ended when my marriage ended. I was lost and had no sense of direction for myself. During one of my sessions with my divorce coach, we discussed that while it didn't seem like it at the moment, all of the heartbreak and what I had experienced actually wasn't for me. Initially I thought that was blasphemous, I felt like if this experience wasn't for me then why did I experience it? It didn't make sense. Well, my faith made me realize that God makes no mistakes so in going through this experience it only made me stronger and allowed me to accept the challenge of going from victim to victor and from wounded to healed.

It was my experience that allowed me to write this book for you. Let me give you an example: There's a well-known '90s female rapper who stepped onto the music scene and worked hard to make a name for herself. Her style, craft and music left an impression and paved the way for many female rappers to follow. While she didn't get the flowers and recognition she deserved, many still idolize her and can credit their success to the path she created! This made me realize that although what I went through wasn't all sunshine and roses, it was definitely in God's plan for me to help you. The disruption in my life wasn't accidental! I needed to go through what I went through to be of service to other women who are feeling stuck and have no idea on how to heal. I want you to know that you too can turn your pain into purpose and your trials into triumphs. You've cried enough tears, and you've suffered enough. It is now time for your own breakthrough.

Depending on where you are on your journey, you may be all in and ready to commit to your healing. On the flip side, you may still be feeling stuck and not quite ready. Well, take it from me--it will get better, but you have to be fully committed to your healing. I knew I owed it to myself and my children to work on my happiness and healing when my brokenness started to affect other areas of my life. If you're not feeling good mind, body, and spirit, then those feelings of angst will eventually spill over into how you're mothering your children and other areas of your life. Stop and think about it for a moment: Where are you right now? What is holding you back from healing? Is where you are right now allowing you to be your best self? Are you ready to discover and walk in your purpose? If you're genuinely ready, then you must do the work.

Right now, you may need to hear the truth instead of what you want to hear. The gift and curse of being girlfriends with me is my transparency. I've never been the friend to pacify you. I'm always going to tell you the hard truths which may sometimes be a tough pill to swallow. If you're going to be the best version of you then you need to take responsibility for the part you played in your marriage. Make peace with it and let it go. Yes, I said it! Think about how your actions played a part in the demise of your marriage or how you allowed yourself to stay in an unhappy marriage. Regardless of the outcome or circumstances, remember it takes two. In no way am I telling you to excuse your ex's actions, but this process is about you.

My purpose isn't to help your ex heal because that's his/her burden to bear. My focus is you! When I gained clarity about my part in what went wrong in my marriage, I learned so much about what not to do in the future and how to be a better woman. This is crucial to not only my healing, but the partner I'll be in a new relationship. Be the captain of your life and take ownership of your emotions, livelihood, and your happiness. While divorce is like driving over a huge pothole on the road, the other side will be smooth once you take control of that wheel! Don't give anyone or anything that much power over your happiness.

Get real with yourself and understand that:

1. Aside from your hurt, there are great things and great people in your life. Find solace and gratitude in the things or people who are positive entities in your life.

2. Spending some time alone for self-care is vital!

3. Journaling, reading, meditating, and exercising can all help your healing. They all are good for your mind, body, and soul.

4. It's now or never, so begin working on your goals and all the things you aspire to do.

5. If certain people or things in your life, or even social media are triggering you then do something about it.

6. It is your job to make yourself feel purposeful. Adding a mate to the mix should be the icing on the cake, not the batter!

7. Not everyone can heal on their own, seek professional help or a support group if needed.

No matter your faith or beliefs, remember that stress, anger and hurt can affect so many aspects of your life. I know this to be true, because I allowed all of the above to get in the way of my mental health and happiness. I want to encourage you to be open to the possibility of seeking professional help if that is a part of your belief system. Joining a women's group and surrounding yourself with others who can relate will also be helpful. Seeking help was the best investment that I could have ever made in myself. I had invested so much in my marriage, so much so that I felt like after my divorce I had nothing else to give. Between divorce coaching, therapy and joining a community of empowering women, I learned and grew tremendously. Through each of these experiences I became more intentional about working on the following aspects of my life:

- forgiveness
- my values
- self-worth
- confidence
- finances
- relationship with my children
- career
- writing
- most of all, my peace.

EPILOGUE

My divorce had left me feeling broken, angry, resentful, and stressed, which is all to be expected when going through such a major shift in life. I was living day by day without any real direction or plan in place to heal. What I did know was that I was tired; tired of pretending that I was okay when I wasn't. I had accepted that life as I knew it didn't exist anymore, so it was up to me to build a new one. Looking at my divorce from a more positive angle allowed me to let go and move forward. Remember that before you were a wife you were a woman. It's important that you remember who that woman is or find her altogether.

Divorce did a number on my self-esteem. It undoubtedly transformed me into someone I could no longer recognize in the mirror. I needed to really sit alone for some time and do some soul searching. This process was ugly but definitely what I needed! I had to stop asking the question, "Why me?" If you plan on moving forward in your healing, you too are going to have to change your mindset. Begin asking yourself, "How can I use my divorce to become an even better version of who I am?" If you are able to do this and consistently do the work, you are on your way to growing and prospering in more ways than you could ever imagine. Your marriage is only a chapter in your life, not the end of the book. Now it's time to lay the foundation for the next chapter.

You may be wondering where you should start. Start with thinking about your strengths and the things that you're good at. As women, we are so quick to ramble off a list of what we don't like about ourselves or areas that need growth, but how often do we acknowledge our strengths or what we do love about ourselves? One book that helped me through my strength finding process was StrengthsFinder 2.0 by Tom Rath. Based upon years of research, his organization came up with this process that suggests that individuals are most productive and become their authentic selves when they are able to own their strengths and skills. Each and every one of us has talents, knowledge and skills. It is this combination of core qualities that makes up our uniqueness, allowing us to master and take on the challenges that come in life. As I looked at my strengths and skills, I rediscovered my true purpose was in my writing and mentoring of others. Sharing my story through blogging not only gave me a platform to express myself, but for other women who were going through similar issues, particularly those who were able to relate and/or gain courage to start their own healing journey. What started out as a form of self-therapy eventually turned into therapy for others.

I knew I was healing when I committed to rebuilding myself. For me this meant, doing things that not only made me happy, but also what made me uncomfortable. It also meant living unapologetically in peace on a consistent and daily basis. This will be a crucial benefit to your healing on so many levels. Part of practicing peace for me meant being conscious of the conversations I had with people and the energy I allowed around me. If it was going to compromise my peace, I knew I wanted no parts of it. I was also able to take inventory of my inner core, which allowed me to become more self-confident and let go of a lot of pain that I had no idea I was still holding on to.

My self-care routines focused more on my emotional, mental, and physical well-being rather than on material and frivolous things. Rebuilding is way more than putting on new clothes, going out and partying or jumping back onto the dating scene to forget the pain. This is a process that starts from the inside, understanding who you are, who you want to be and never settling for the same pain. Are you ready to write your next chapter and rebuild yourself? The next chapter after my divorce is still being written, but the beauty of it is that I am the author! Healing has no timeline. The goal shouldn't be to heal as fast as you can but to do so as thoroughly as you can. Recognize where you are and focus on moving forward. Throw on your cape and save yourself! Your healing and the next chapter of your life depends on it.

RESOURCES

Munroe, Myles. *Single Married Separated And Life After Divorce Daily Study*. (United States: Destiny Image Publishers, 2004)

Rath, Tom. StrengthsFinder 2.0. Simon and Schuster, 2007.

Roberts, Sarah Jakes. Don't Settle for Safe. Thomas Nelson, 2017.

ABOUT THE AUTHOR

Renee Jackson was born and raised in Brooklyn, New York and has been an educator for over a decade. While being an educator has been rewarding, Renee's greatest love is being a mother to her two daughters. Her hobbies growing up included reading, writing, and tutoring. In pursuit of her childhood dream of teaching, she attended St. John's University and obtained a Bachelor's in Education with a concentration in English. She then received two Masters, one in Literacy (from Hunter College) and another in School Leadership (from Touro College). Renee realized she was tired of feeling broken, lost, and uncertain of who she was as a woman after going through some life changing experiences which included her mother having a severe stroke which left her physically incapacitated, going through a divorce and left with the uncertainty of how she would raise her two daughters as a single mother.

Renee could have allowed her pain and trials to defeat her and dictate her path. Instead, she went on a path of healing that not only saved her life but led to the breaking of generational curses that her daughters would not be subject to. This journey led Renee to blogging about her healing and using this self-therapy to help other women who were suffering in silence, to embark on their own journey of healing. While being an educator has been fulfilling, Renee knew early on in her life that having a passion for something doesn't necessarily mean it is your purpose. The pain she experienced, and her healing journey led Renee on a mission to accept her purpose. Her mission is to help other women heal wounds from past relationships and provide them with encouragement, tools, and empowerment to overcome their own adversities.

Would you like to connect with Renee or inquire about coaching? Follow her on social media or visit her online:

Instagram @reneethecoach
Website: healingwoundsofdivorce.com
Book Purchasing: healingwoundsofdivorcethebook.com
Email: healingwoundsofdivorce@gmail.com

www.ingramcontent.com/pod-product-compliance
Lightning Source LLC
LaVergne TN
LVHW050610100826
845148LV00015B/3214

* 9 7 8 0 5 7 8 9 8 5 1 1 4 *